Home for the Spring Festival

Before You Read

This story is about the country of China, its culture, its customs, and its most important festival.

A. Spring Festival. Look at the mind map. Then complete the sentences with the correct form of the underlined words.

1. _____ some stories, a monster called *nian* would come around people's houses on New Year's Eve, so people would try to scare him away.
2. In China, people set off _____ when they open a new business.
3. Another important holiday in China is the Dragon Boat _____, which is in May or June.
4. The Mid-Autumn Festival is _____ by people eating mooncakes.
5. Our friends and _____ are important to us.
6. Today, many people still find themselves drawn to traditional _____, as these help them connect with their past and culture.

---

¹**dragon:** a large, imaginary creature which can fly and is quite powerful
²**parade:** people walking down the street wearing special clothes to celebrate a festival or holiday
³**lunar:** related to the moon

B. New Year, A New Zodiac Animal. Look at the table and the photos in this reader. Then answer the questions below.

The Chinese Zodiac[4]
With the Chinese zodiac, every year has a different animal.

	Animal	Year	Character
	rat	2020	clever, friendly, lucky, confident
	ox	2021	hard-working, patient, simple, loving
	tiger	2022	strong, not afraid, loves adventure
	rabbit	2023	kind, gentle, cares about the feelings of others
	dragon	2024	full of life, clever, wants to do what is right
	snake	2025	clever, charming, patient, gifted, talented at art
	horse	2026	has a warm heart, doesn't give up, easy to be with
	goat	2027	polite, kind, loves family
	monkey	2028	clever, lively, kind
	rooster	2029	likes to dress up, happy, doesn't like to wait
	dog	2030	stands by others, not afraid, full of life, honest
	pig	2031	giving, stands by others, has a warm heart

1. What do you know about the Spring Festival, also known as the Chinese New Year?
2. Have you ever celebrated the Spring Festival? If so, how?
3. Why do you think the Chinese people see the Spring Festival as so important?
4. How do New Year's celebrations in other countries differ from the Spring Festival?

[4] **zodiac:** *a system related to the stars or the calendar where people are given a sign or animal, and that is supposed to decide their personality and fortune*

Every year at around the same time, it looks as if everyone in China is on the move. In all the big cities, the train stations, roads, and airports are packed with people going back to their **hometowns**[5] for the Spring Festival. For example, in 2019, the Spring Festival saw 410 million trips by railway, 2.46 **billion**[6] by road, and 73 million by air. The Spring Festival, known in many other countries around the world as Chinese New Year, is celebrated over a few days between January 21 and February 20. The reason the date changes is because it is the new year according to the lunar calendar, which is based on the cycles of the moon rather than the time it takes the Earth to go around the sun. In modern China, many people live far away from their hometowns, so they long to go home and see their loved ones. In addition, as the longest holiday in China, for many people it is the one time of the year when everyone in the family is able to travel home to be together. Of course, as it is the New Year, it is also a good time to say goodbye to the old, and welcome the new.

Track 1

[5] **hometown**: the place where one was born or lived as a child
[6] **billion**: 1,000,000,000

After they get home, many people join in preparing for the Spring Festival. For example, they put red paper cuttings on the windows. These may be of lucky fish or it may be the Chinese word for spring, the zodiac animal for that year, or the character *fu* (福), which means good **fortune**.[7] You see the color red everywhere, because to the Chinese people it means happiness and good fortune. On both sides of their front door, they put a New Year's **couplet**,[8] written in gold or black on long pieces of red paper, giving good wishes for the year. On the door itself, they often put a large piece of red paper with the character *fu* on it.

[7]**fortune**: luck, money, wealth
[8]**couplet**: two lines of poetry often of equal length

Main Idea

1. What is the main idea of the paragraph on page 4?
2. Why do so many people travel during this time?

The day before the New Year, the family will join together to prepare that night's meal, the family dinner, which for many people is the most important family meal of the year. The kinds of food will be different from family to family, but some dishes are more popular in some areas. Many families have fish, as the Chinese word for fish is *yu*, which is a play on words for **abundant**,[9] and so eating fish means that they wish to have an abundant year. Another popular dish is *niangao*. This is a sweet cake, which is eaten because its name is a play on the Chinese word for better year.

[9] **abundant**: more than enough

In northern China, the most popular New Year's food is *jiaozi*, **dumplings**[10] which are often filled with meat and vegetables. Of course, *jiaozi* is famous as a food that people in northern China eat all year round. However, having them at New Year is special because often the whole family will spend some time sitting at a table making that night's *jiaozi* together. This custom comes from the Chinese characters for *jiaozi*. Part of the character for *jiao* means to cross over, while the character for *zi* can mean the time between 11 p.m. and 1 a.m. So, the word *jiaozi* is said to mean the crossing over from one year to the next, or saying goodbye to the past and welcoming the future.

[10] **dumpling:** *a ball of food cooked in water or soup*

After the New Year's Eve meal, the family will often watch TV together. Many watch the **CCTV**[11] **Gala**,[12] which ends after midnight. Then, people set off fireworks from nearly every garden and street. This is done to drive away bad **spirits**[13] and bad luck. It can go on for as long as an hour, though in many places setting off fireworks is not allowed in order to protect the environment. Finally, it is quiet as everyone goes to bed. However, some people wake up early and light more fireworks to welcome the first day of the new year.

[11] **CCTV**: China Central Television
[12] **gala**: a special event, usually with famous people
[13] **spirit**: a ghost or a being from another non-physical world

The Chinese New Year would not be complete without visiting relatives, usually starting on the second day of the new year. For people who are married, the first stop will usually be the wife's parents, then other relatives are visited in turn. Everywhere one goes, one hears the words *Guonian hao!* or *Xinnian kuaile!* (both mean Happy New Year!).

Of course, visitors should always bring a gift for everyone they visit. Children and young people usually get a red envelope with some money. The envelope should never be opened in front of the person who gave it. While in the past, red envelopes were nearly always given by an aunt, uncle, or grandparent to a younger family member, now nearly anyone of any age can give or receive a red envelope. Some companies even give them to their workers. These red envelopes are so popular that you can send them with money digitally to your loved ones, using your phone.

Match

Match the Chinese words with their English meanings.

1. *fu*
2. *yu*
3. *niangao*
4. *jiaozi*
5. *Xin nian kuai le!*

a. Chinese dumplings
b. Happy New Year!
c. sweet cake; better year
d. good fortune
e. fish; abundant

At the end of the holiday, it is time for people to return to work. The train stations, roads, and airports are once again packed with people going back to the big cities. As the weather begins to warm and spring arrives, flowers start to open up, and the new hope and good fortune people wished for at New Year's begin to show in the season's loveliness.

My own first experience of the Chinese New Year was very much like that described above. I just had a baby, and since we were far away from home, a Chinese friend named Mei helped us out. Mei's husband worked as a chef in another city, so Mei and her daughter rarely saw him. Then during the Spring Festival he was able to come home for a few days. Since we had a large kitchen and no relatives in China, we asked them to spend New Year's Eve at our house. Mei's husband spent the day cooking holiday food, including a fish so large that we had trouble finding a plate big enough for it.

We also made pork *jiaozi* together. During the meal, I got a *jiaozi* which was sweet. This is supposed to mean good fortune for the next year. Then we watched the CCTV Gala on TV. On the stroke of midnight, we went outside to set off fireworks. Though it was a bitterly cold Northeast China night, many people were outside lighting fireworks with us. While the food was wonderful, everything was plain and simple. What I remember most was the friendship we shared together that night so many years ago.

No matter where in the world you live, or whether you call it the Spring Festival or the Chinese New Year, this is a celebration of family, reunion, and hope for the New Year.

CCTV Gala

Making jiaozi together

What Do You Think?

1. What do many Chinese people wish for in the new year?
2. What do you wish for in the new year?
3. Do you think that there are ways you can become lucky or have good fortune? What are they?

After You Read

A. Multiple Choice. Answer the questions below by choosing A, B, C, or D.

1. In the first paragraph, on page 4, when it says, "everyone in China is on the move," what does "on the move" mean?
   A. being busy
   B. making decisions
   C. feeling emotions
   D. traveling

2. A good heading for the paragraph on page 8 is:
   A. New Year's Dinner: Special Food for a Special Time
   B. Foods with Good Meanings for the New Year
   C. Foods Families Prepare Together for the New Year
   D. Different Foods for Different Areas of China

3. For the Spring Festival, Chinese people like to eat foods _____.
   A. which only include fish
   B. which mean good luck
   C. which are sweet
   D. which they help make together with their family

4. In the passage, what do some people do using a mobile app during the Spring Festival?
   A. watch the CCTV Gala
   B. send a digital red envelope
   C. take photos of food
   D. call friends and wish them a happy new year

5. Why was the author of the passage considered lucky on New Year's Eve?
   A. She just had a baby.
   B. Her friend's husband cooked her a wonderful meal.
   C. She got a sweet *jiaozi*.
   D. She shared some good friendship.

B. Complete the Notes. Complete the notes below with words from the passage.

Spring Festival

People go home	2019: 410 million trips by (1) _____, 2.46 billion by road, and 73 million by air
Chinese (2) _____	celebrated sometime between Jan. 21 and Feb. 20, according to lunar (3) _____
Longest holiday	it is a time when many people usually (4) _____
Customs	everything red, meaning (5) _____ & (6) _____; red paper cuttings; New Year's (7) _____ on both sides of the front door; red paper with fu on the front door
Typical foods	fish, meaning abundant; niangao, meaning better year; northern China, jiaozi, meaning (8) _____
After dinner	CCTV Gala; fireworks to drive away (9) _____
Later	visit relatives; red (10) _____; everyone says Xin nian kuai le! or Guo nian hao!

C. Answer the questions. Use information from the passage to answer the questions below.

1. What impressed the author most about his own first Chinese New Year's experience?
2. What does the Spring Festival tell us about the kinds of things Chinese people value?
3. What other Chinese festivals do you know about or have you experienced? What can you tell about them?

The Lantern Festival

🎧 **Track 2**

While most people think the Chinese New Year's celebration goes on for only one day, by custom it is a fifteen-day celebration, and some of these days have their own festivals. The most important of these is the festival on the 15th day of the Chinese New Year celebration, the Lantern Festival.

It is not really clear how the Lantern Festival started. What is known is that the festival is over 2,000 years old. In one old story, an emperor ordered people to light lanterns to honor Buddha. Much later, people began to carry around red paper lanterns with pieces of paper attached that had riddles written on them. In many cities, people come together in parks with their lanterns, and it is a game to walk around and try to solve each other's riddles.

During the Tang Dynasty (618-907), the festival became so important that it went on for three days, and rules stopping people going out at night were lifted. Everyone was allowed to join in the fun and the Lantern Festival became the one time of the year when single women could get out of the house at night. For this reason, the festival became linked with dating and love.

During the Lantern Festival, many people eat *tangyuan* or *yuanxiao*. In fact, eating *yuanxiao* is so popular that another name for the Lantern Festival is the Yuanxiao Festival. *Tangyuan* and *yuanxiao* are quite similar, and some people even say they are the same food. Both are dumplings made of rice flour. While they are often filled with something sweet, like sweet beans, they can be filled with a variety of ingredients and are sometimes salty. They are usually served with the water they were cooked in. These foods are most often eaten at home with the family on the day of the Lantern Festival.

Of course, an important part of the Lantern Festival is the lanterns themselves. Some cities try to have the largest, most beautiful lanterns around, of all different kinds of shapes and sizes. During this time of year, you can see streets lined with lanterns and parks that are seas of lanterns, making everyone feel festive and happy.

Word Count: 364
Time: _____

Vocabulary List

abundant *(8, 15, 21)*
according to *(2, 4)*
allow *(12, 22)*
based on *(4)*
billion *(4, 21)*
bitterly *(18)*
celebrate *(2, 3, 4, 21)*
celebration *(3, 18, 22)*
character *(3, 6, 11)*
charming *(3)*
confident *(3)*
couplet *(6)*
custom *(2, 11, 21, 22)*
dragon *(2, 3)*
dumpling *(11, 15, 23)*
Earth *(4)*
environment *(12)*
experience *(17, 21)*
festival *(2, 3, 4, 6, 17, 18, 20, 21, 22, 23)*
fireworks *(2, 12, 18, 21)*
fortune *(3, 6, 15, 17, 18, 19)*
friendship *(18, 20)*

gala *(12, 18, 20, 21)*
gentle *(3)*
goat *(3)*
happiness *(6)*
hometown *(4)*
honest *(3)*
in addition *(4)*
lunar *(2, 4, 21)*
parade *(2)*
plain *(18)*
pork *(18)*
protect *(12)*
rarely *(17)*
rather *(4)*
relative *(2, 14, 17, 21)*
spirit *(12)*
talented *(3)*
though *(12, 18)*
trouble *(17)*
typical *(21)*
zodiac *(3, 6)*